Thoroughbred Horses

by Grace Hansen

Abdo
HORSES
Kids

abdopublishing.com

Published by Abdo Kids, a division of ABDO, P.O. Box 398166, Minneapolis, Minnesota 55439.

Copyright © 2017 by Abdo Consulting Group, Inc. International copyrights reserved in all countries. No part of this book may be reproduced in any form without written permission from the publisher.

Printed in the United States of America, North Mankato, Minnesota.

102016

012017

THIS BOOK CONTAINS RECYCLED MATERIALS

Photo Credits: Depositphotos Enterprise, iStock, Shutterstock, ©Stefan Holm p.15 / Shutterstock.com

Production Contributors: Teddy Borth, Jennie Forsberg, Grace Hansen

Design Contributors: Dorothy Toth, Laura Mitchell

Publisher's Cataloging in Publication Data

Names: Hansen, Grace, author.

Title: Thoroughbred horses / by Grace Hansen.

Description: Minneapolis, Minnesota : Abdo Kids, 2017 | Series: Horses | Includes bibliographical references and index.

Identifiers: LCCN 2016944094 | ISBN 9781680809305 (lib. bdg.) | ISBN 9781680796407 (ebook) | ISBN 9781680797077 (Read-to-me ebook)

Subjects: LCSH: Thoroughbred horses--Juvenile literature.

Classification: DDC 636.1/32--dc23

LC record available at http://lccn.loc.gov/2016944094

Table of Contents

Thoroughbred Horses

The thoroughbred is a gifted horse. Its long legs and lean body make it a racing machine!

4

A thoroughbred has a long neck. Its back is short and curved.

The **profile** of the head is straight. The nostrils are large. This helps with breathing. The horse's big eyes are set far apart.

9

These horses come in many colors. **Bay**, black, and chestnut are common. They can have markings on their faces and ankles.

These horses are taller than most horse breeds. They grow up to 17 **hands** tall. Other horses, on average, are 15.2 hands.

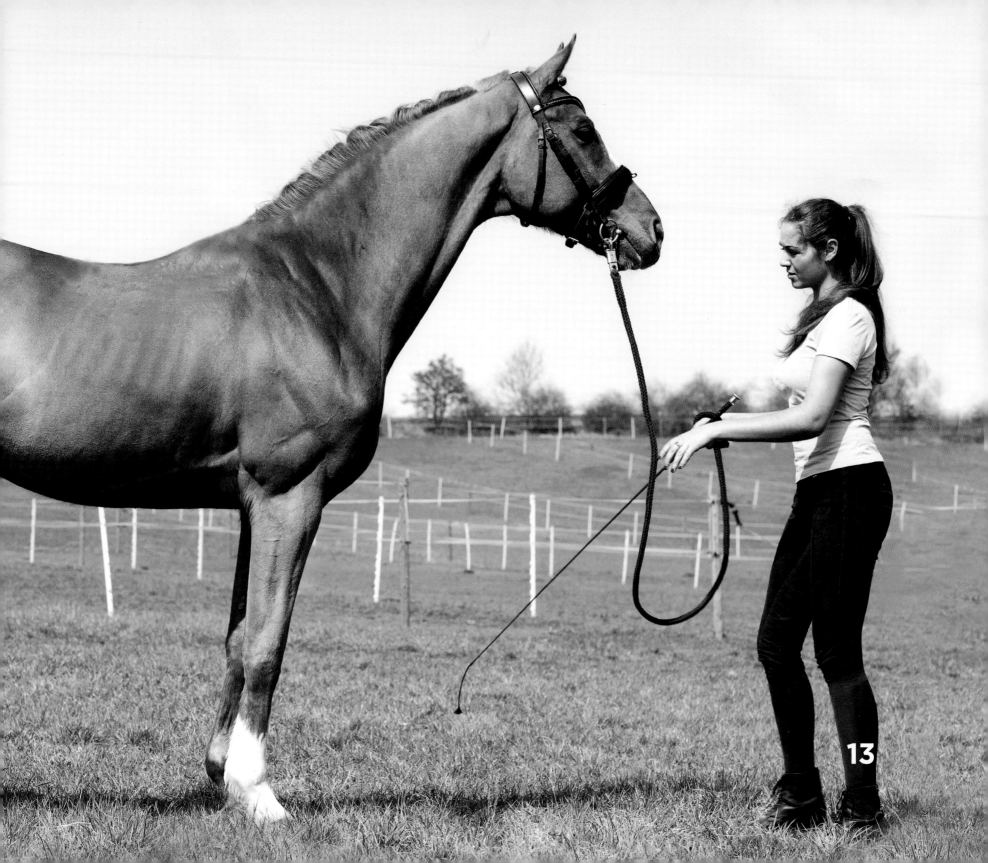

Racers!

Thoroughbreds are known best for racing. They can gallop more than 40 miles an hour (64 km/h)! People love going to the races to cheer them on.

This breed can be trained for other things, too. They do well in jumping. Many are used for the sport polo.

Personality & Training

Thoroughbreds are hot-blooded horses. This means they have lots of energy. They can also be sensitive.

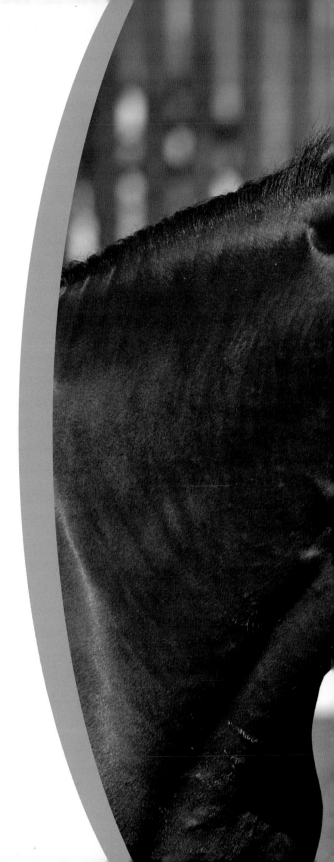

Training this horse is no easy job. Someone with experience must train it. When trained well, this horse is unbeatable!

More Facts

- Secretariat was one of the greatest thoroughbred racehorses of all time. He won 16 out of the 21 races he ran. His fastest speed was 40.18 mph (64.66 km/h).

- The fastest thoroughbred is Winning Brew. In 2008, she was clocked at 43.97 mph (70.76 km/h).

- Because these horses often work so hard, they need to eat lots of food. They can eat 20 pounds (9 kg) of hay per day!

Glossary

bay – reddish brown.

hands – a unit of length (1 hand is equal to 4 inches or 10.16 cm) and used primarily for measuring the height of horses from the ground to the top of the shoulders.

polo – a game played on horseback between two teams, the object being to score two points by driving a wooden ball into a goal using a mallet.

profile – the side view of a head.

23

Index

abdokids.com

Use this code to log on to abdokids.com and access crafts, games, videos and more!

Abdo Kids Code:
HTK9305